Sea
Anemones

creatures of the sea

Sea Anemones

Kris Hirschmann

KIDHAVEN PRESS

An imprint of Thomson Gale, a part of The Thomson Corporation

THOMSON

GALE

Detroit • New York • San Francisco • San Diego
New Haven, Conn. • Waterville, Maine • London • Munich

For Steve P., best friend of the manatee.

© 2005 Thomson Gale, a part of The Thomson Corporation.

Thomson and Star Logo are trademarks and Gale and KidHaven Press are registered trademarks used herein under license.

For more information, contact
KidHaven Press
27500 Drake Rd.
Farmington Hills, MI 48331-3535
Or you can visit our Internet site at http://www.gale.com

LIBRARY OF CONGRESS CATALOGING-IN-PUBLICATION DATA
Hirschmann, Kris, 1967–
Sea anemones / by Kris Hirschmann.
p. cm. — (Creatures of the sea)
Includes bibliographical references and index.
Contents: Sea anemone basics—Sea anemone reproduction—Feeding and defense—Living together.
ISBN 0-7377-3009-9 (hardcover : alk. paper)
1. Sea anemones—Juvenile literature. I. Title.
QL377.C7H57 2005
593.6—dc22
2005000739

Printed in the United States of America

Table of Contents

Introduction

Flower Animals

With their stemlike bodies and colorful, waving **tentacles**, sea anemones look a lot like underwater flowers. It is no surprise, then, that people once thought these animals were a type of underwater plant. The sea anemone's common name even comes from a land-living family of flowers, the anemones, whose slender petals are similar to the delicate tentacles of their ocean-dwelling look-alikes.

Today, scientists know that sea anemones are not plants at all. They are simple animals that live, eat, breathe, and reproduce in ways typical of all living creatures. In terms of appearance, sea anemones are the flowers of the sea. The name of their scientific class, **Anthozoa**, even refers to this fact. The word

Sea anemones like these jewel anemones are colorful underwater animals that look like flowers.

anthozoa comes from Greek words meaning "flower animal."

Where conditions are good, sea anemones often live together in vast numbers. They spread out across the ocean floor to create stunning carpets of color. Waving back and forth in the ocean currents, the anemone colonies look like mountain meadows that have suddenly found themselves on the seabed. These underwater flower gardens are one of the most spectacular sights in the undersea world. They are also living proof of the sea anemone's success. These creatures may be simple, but they have everything they need to thrive in the ocean environment.

1

Sea Anemone Basics

The underwater world is in constant motion as colorful fish dart from place to place, sea grasses bend and sway, and hard-shelled creatures creep slowly across the seafloor. Adding to the commotion are animals called sea anemones, whose many tentacles wiggle and wave in the ocean currents. Sea anemones are very simple creatures, but they are fascinating members of the ocean community nonetheless.

There are about 900 types of sea anemones worldwide. These animals are closely related to corals, jellyfish, and hydras. All sea anemones belong to the scientific order **Actiniaria**, which comes from a Greek word meaning "ray." This name refers to the raylike tentacles sticking out from a sea anemone's central body.

Colorful fish swim over a bed of anemones with purple tentacles near the island of Fiji.

Where Sea Anemones Live

Sea anemones generally are saltwater creatures, although a few species can live in brackish (partly salty) water. Most species prefer tropical areas. However, sea anemones can be found in all the oceans of the world, from the warm waters near the equator to the coldest polar seas. In some chilly areas, including the Antarctic seabed, anemones are so abundant that they form enormous living carpets on the seafloor.

Sea anemones can be found not only in every ocean, but at every depth as well. These creatures are very common on shallow coral reefs and along shorelines around the world, but they are equally common in waters as deep as 33,000 feet (10,000m). They have even been found living around deep-sea vents, which continually belch hot, chemical-rich water into the ocean. Most sea creatures could not survive in these areas, but anemones seem to do just fine in these challenging conditions.

Coastal anemones do not have to deal with extreme depths or conditions. They do, however, need to keep themselves safe and damp when the tide goes out. For this reason, shallow-living sea anemones usually settle in tidal pools or other places that stay wet all the time. Some sea anemone species can live out of the water for short periods. These species may live in dark cracks or beneath overhanging rocks that protect them from the sun's rays.

Wherever they are found, most sea anemones attach themselves to hard surfaces, such as rocks or coral. A few species, including the daisy anemone, burrow into sand or mud and leave only the top parts of their bodies exposed. Members of one family, called the **minyads**, float near the sea surface and travel wherever the currents take them.

The Sea Anemone Body

All sea anemones share certain physical features. The main body of a sea anemone is called the **column**. The column is basically a tube with a hollow interior called the **gastrovascular cavity**. This cavity serves as the sea anemone's stomach.

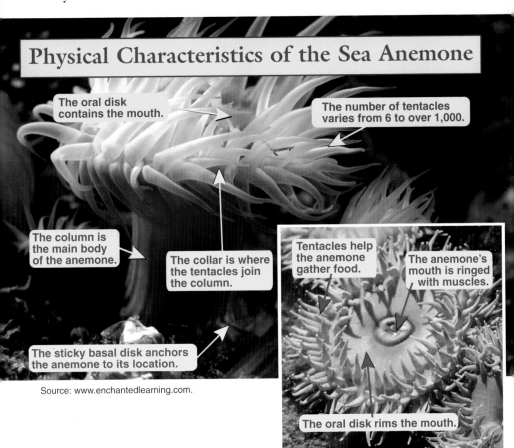

Physical Characteristics of the Sea Anemone

The oral disk contains the mouth.

The number of tentacles varies from 6 to over 1,000.

The column is the main body of the anemone.

The collar is where the tentacles join the column.

Tentacles help the anemone gather food.

The anemone's mouth is ringed with muscles.

The sticky basal disk anchors the anemone to its location.

The oral disk rims the mouth.

Source: www.enchantedlearning.com.

The bottom of the column is generally attached to a solid surface by a sticky pad called the **basal disk**. The top of the column ends in a flat, fleshy area called the **oral disk**. The oral disk is smooth, with a muscle-ringed opening in the center. This opening is the sea anemone's mouth. Because the mouth is the only way into or out of the sea anemone's body, it is also the opening through which waste products are released.

Fringing the oral disk are the sea anemone's flexible tentacles. Some species have as few as six tentacles, while others may have a thousand or more. The largest tentacles are usually found in the middle, with the others becoming smaller and smaller toward the edges of the column. Where the tentacles meet the column, there is a loose fold of flesh called the **collar**. When the tentacles are fully extended, the collar drapes downward around the column.

Sizes, Shapes, and Colors

Sea anemones come in many different sizes. The smallest anemones measure just a fraction of an inch (a few millimeters) across the column. The largest may be more than 3 feet (1m) from side to side. The world's biggest species is the Merten's sea anemone, which is found on Australia's Great Barrier Reef.

Body shape also varies from species to species. A sea anemone's column, for example, can be tall or short, slim or squat. It can be one uniform width from top to bottom, or it may bulge in places. The tentacles,

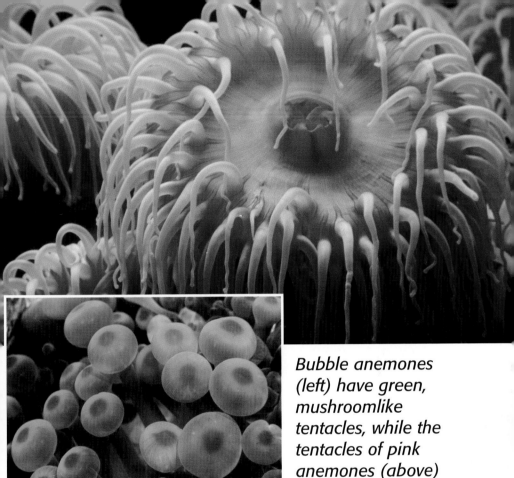

Bubble anemones (left) have green, mushroomlike tentacles, while the tentacles of pink anemones (above) are long and thin.

too, are shaped differently from one sea anemone to another. They may be short and delicate, as in the common plumose anemone, or long and thick, as in the snakelocks anemone. Some species, including the club-tipped anemone and the giant anemone, have round, fleshy bulbs at the ends of their tentacles.

Color is yet another way to tell sea anemones apart. The most common colors are yellow, green, and blue, but sea anemones occur in practically every color imaginable, including red, pink, white, brown, orange, and more. Different parts of the body may be different colors. The tricolor anemone, for example, has a brown column with cream streaks; a yellow, red, and pink oral disk; and white or orange tentacles. The corkscrew anemone has see-through tentacles with whitish corkscrew-like markings. These and other colorful species tend to be found in warm, shallow waters. In contrast, deepwater species are often drab.

The bodies of many shallow-water anemones, like these purple anemones, are very brightly colored.

On the Move

Since many sea anemones stay in one place for long periods, location can be another clue to an anemone's identity. However, this identification method is not foolproof. Although sea anemones do not move around a lot, they are not fixed in place. They simply cling to things with their basal disks rather than being cemented to them, like their relatives, the corals. When a sea anemone wants to go somewhere, it releases its hold and sets off across the ocean floor.

Most sea anemones travel by creeping along on their basal disks. Using this method, an anemone's maximum speed is about 2 to 3 inches (5 to 7.5cm) per hour. Such high speeds, however, are unusual. A sea anemone on the move usually travels just a fraction of an inch (a few millimeters) per day.

Some anemones have different ways of moving from place to place. A few species bend their bodies into upside-down "U" shapes and creep along like inchworms. Others move by somersaulting along the seafloor. Some can even swim short distances by waving their tentacles or thrashing their columns back and forth. The movement is not graceful, but it does allow them to get from one place to another.

Anemones have no bones to support their bodies and muscles, so to travel or to move in any other way a sea anemone uses water pressure. It fills its central body cavity with water, then shuts its mouth

With its mouth tightly closed to hold in water, an anemone inches along the seafloor.

tight to prevent the water from escaping. When squeezed, the trapped water holds the anemone's flesh rigid and gives its muscles something to pull against. Without this remarkable system, sea anemones could not control their movement, let alone travel anywhere. A temporary water skeleton is one of the many features that help sea anemones to survive and thrive in the ocean environment.

Sea Anemone Reproduction

There is no easy way to tell a sea anemone's age. However, scientists believe that most sea anemones are long-lived creatures. If conditions are good, anemones probably live for decades, and individuals of some species may even live for hundreds of years—or perhaps more. In 1996, tests suggested that some large deep-sea anemones collected in the Bahamas were more than 2,000 years old. If this is true, these anemones are the oldest ocean animals ever discovered.

During its long lifetime, a sea anemone's most important job is to keep the species alive by creating new sea anemones. Unlike most animals, which have just one method of reproduction, sea anemones have several ways to carry out this vital task.

Spawning

One way sea anemones reproduce is by **spawning**, or releasing eggs and sperm into the water. In most sea anemone species, an individual is both male and female, which means it can make both eggs and sperm. Younger anemones usually act as males. Older anemones usually act as females. This probably happens because it takes more energy to make eggs than sperm. Older sea anemones tend to be bigger and stronger, so they perform the more difficult job.

At certain times of the year, environmental cues such as water temperature, moon phases, and tidal cycles tell sea anemones that it is almost time to spawn. In response to these cues, the anemones start developing eggs or sperm inside their bodies. Before long it is time for the actual spawning to take place. All of the individuals in an area release their eggs and sperm at the same time. The males seem to smoke as sperm leave their bodies in a grayish cloud, and soon the water is thick with spawn. If the eggs and sperm meet in the water, the eggs will be fertilized. Soon they develop into young sea anemones called **larvae**.

Some species have a slightly different way of creating larvae. Males still release their sperm into the water when spawning time arrives, but females keep their eggs within their bodies. The eggs are fertilized when the female takes in water containing sperm. The eggs develop into larvae inside the female's body. In polar regions, some sea anemones keep their larvae in brood pouches on the outside of the column until the larvae are big enough to begin life on their own.

Life as a Larva

A sea anemone larva is called a **planula**. In its early stages, a planula is nothing but a ball of cells. Each cell has a hair sticking out of it. These tiny hairs beat rhythmically to push the planula through the water.

Surrounded by red sea urchins, a male anemone (circled) releases a cloud of sperm into the water.

As soon as it can swim, a planula enters the plankton, which is a drifting community of microscopic plants and animals. The planula floats on the ocean currents, moving farther and farther away from its parents. As it floats, it swims through the plankton and tries to catch other tiny animals to eat. It also tries not to get eaten itself. If the planula avoids danger, it gets bigger and stronger. Its body also changes, developing adult internal structures.

Pictured is a magnified view of plankton, the floating community of microscopic plants and animals where anemone larvae live.

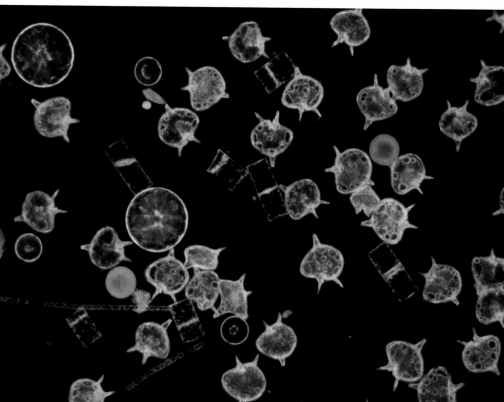

A planula lives in the plankton anywhere from a few days to several weeks. At the end of this time, the planula is big enough and heavy enough to drop from the plankton and settle to the ocean floor. Once it arrives on the bottom, the planula holds on to the seafloor with its tiny mouth pointing upward. It soon grows a ring of tentacles around its mouth, completing its transformation from planula to **polyp**, the name given to all adult sea anemones.

The newly formed polyp is tiny, but it will not be tiny for long. The little anemone will eat and grow, eat and grow. It will sprout more and more tentacles around the edges of its expanding oral disk. Before long the young sea anemone will be a full-fledged adult, ready to spawn and create more sea anemones to populate the oceans.

Reproduction by Splitting

Some sea anemones bypass the spawning process altogether. Instead, they reproduce by **splitting** themselves into two identical animals. Most anemones split vertically. To do this, they use their basal disk to crawl in two opposite directions at the same time. The column stretches until it reaches the breaking point. Then it rips down the center, tearing the original anemone in half. It takes some time for each half to heal and become whole again. Before long, however, there are two healthy sea anemones where once there was only one. Eventually both of these anemones will split, thus producing more and more animals from a single parent.

A few types of anemones do not split vertically. They split horizontally instead, breaking apart halfway up their column. Anemones that use this method of reproduction grow an extra ring of tentacles around the middle section when they are preparing to split. Their bodies then break apart just above the new tentacles. The top part of the anemone tumbles to the seafloor, where it reattaches itself and becomes whole again.

Sea anemones that are created by splitting are exact clones of each other. Over time and many generations, splitting sea anemones can create enormous colonies of identical individuals. All of the sea anemones in these colonies look the same, and they cluster very close together. These traits make clone colonies easy to identify.

Regeneration

In addition to spawning and splitting, sea anemones can also reproduce through a process called **regeneration**. This means that a new sea anemone can grow from a very small piece of an old anemone. It does not matter whether the piece has all the organs and parts necessary for survival. As the piece gets bigger, it will grow everything it needs.

Regeneration can happen any time a sea anemone loses part of its body. In warm areas, for example, certain sea anemones drop tentacles, which attach

These snakelocks anemones are clones of each other. They formed when a single anemone split itself in two.

themselves to the ocean floor and develop into new animals. Other sea anemones leave tiny bits of their basal disks behind as they move across the seabed. Each of these tiny bits eventually grows into a new anemone, creating a living trail that marks the path of the original parent.

Like anemones produced through splitting, re-generated anemones are identical clones of their

This plumose anemone shed tiny bits of its basal disk, which have grown into new anemones.

parent. This means, in part, that they are fully functional adults, able to spawn, split, and regenerate on their own. They will do all three things during their long lifetimes, thereby creating new sea anemones and keeping ocean populations strong and healthy.

chapter 3

Feeding and Defense

L ike all ocean animals, sea anemones spend a great deal of time searching for food and eating. Anemones satisfy their appetites with a wide variety of food. Smaller species eat plankton and debris. Larger species are hungry **predators** that will devour fish, crabs, shrimp, worms, and anything else they can catch.

Sea anemones do not have brains. They do, however, have networks of nerves. Using these nerves, a sea anemone can touch, taste, and sense differences in light. With these simple senses, an anemone can catch all the food it needs to survive.

Catching Food

Although sea anemones are hunters, they do not chase their prey. They sit in one place and wait for prey to come to them. A sea anemone waves its tentacles back and forth through the water as it waits. By staying in constant motion, the anemone gives itself the best possible chance of touching any food that wanders past.

Depending on their size, sea anemones may catch food in a couple of ways. Sea anemones that eat small food, such as plankton and organic debris, grab meals with the help of their mucus-covered bodies. Like flypaper, the sticky mucus traps any food particles it touches. Tiny hairs on the tentacles beat in rhythm to create water currents that push the particles away from the anemone's mouth. The particles gather at the tentacle tips. When a good-

An anemone draws the plankton stuck to the ends of its tentacles into its mouth.

size chunk of food has been collected on any tentacle, the sea anemone bends the tentacle inward and drops the tasty packet into its mouth.

Sea anemones that eat larger food, such as fish and worms, have a different way of subduing their prey. These anemones' tentacles are lined with huge numbers of stingers called **nematocysts**. Each nematocyst contains a coiled thread with a barbed end. When anything brushes against an anemone's tentacles, the nematocysts fire their threads like little harpoons. The threads pierce the prey's flesh and begin to inject a poison that is both painful and paralyzing. As the prey struggles, it touches more and more of the anemone's tentacles, thus causing more and more nematocysts to fire. Soon the prey is attached to the anemone by thousands of delicate strands. It is also sluggish from the poison in its system. Helpless and sick, the prey will not fight too hard as it is eaten.

Eating and Digestion

Once prey has been caught and paralyzed, the tentacles carry it to the center of the oral disk. The mouth opens wide so the food can be pushed inside. Since sea anemones cannot chew, anything they eat is swallowed whole.

Inside the anemone's body, the food moves through a short passage into the gut. Stingers in the stomach pierce the prey again and pump more venom into its body to keep it paralyzed. At the same time, digestive juices begin to flow from the walls of the

A hungry pink anemone wraps its tentacles around a butterfly fish.

stomach. These juices bathe the prey and start to break down its flesh. Because the juices are strong, this process happens very quickly. A sea anemone can transform small prey into liquid nourishment within about fifteen minutes. After this process is finished, usable parts are absorbed by the sea anemone. Unusable parts, such as shells and bones, leave the body through the mouth. The sea anemone may also have to spit out rocks, sand, or any other nonfood items it swallowed along with its dinner.

A sea anemone that snags a good meal will not need to eat again for a while. Its tentacles become less sensitive, allowing other creatures to touch the anemone without being stung. When the anemone gets hungry again, however, its nematocysts will return to being deadly. The sea anemone will once again be an eating machine, ready and able to capture nearly any prey it happens to touch.

Sea Anemones as Prey

Because of their stingers, sea anemones do not have many enemies. However, some creatures do prey on anemones. Sea anemone predators include eels, flounder, codfish, and some sea stars. These animals do not seem to be bothered by the sea anemone's barbs or poison and will gladly make a meal of this soft, easy-to-chew creature.

Certain sea slugs called nudibranchs are especially successful predators of sea anemones. A nudibranch can eat its entire body weight in sea anemone flesh in a single day. This animal's throat, stomach, and other internal passages are coated with thick mucus that protects the slug from any unexploded nematocysts it swallows. The nudibranch passes the nematocysts into structures along its own back and uses them to sting other creatures, including anemones. When the stolen nematocysts are used up, the nudibranch eats more anemones to rebuild its supply.

Sea anemones may also be preyed upon by other anemones. If colonies of two different species grow too close to each other, they fight for position. The anemones sting each other repeatedly. After a while the sea anemones seem to reach a compromise, and a narrow, clear strip develops between the colonies. Neither side will enter this neutral zone, and the colonies will stop trying to hurt each other.

Staying Safe

Because nematocysts do not always provide enough protection, sea anemones use a variety of other defenses to keep themselves safe from predators. One defense is simply to hide the tentacles. To do this, anemones pull their tentacles in toward the center of the oral disk. The collar that rings the base of the tentacles then turns inside out and upward. It closes itself tightly around the tentacles, making the sea anemone look like nothing but a fleshy lump. With luck, a predator will not even notice the disguised anemone.

Camouflage is another technique that helps a sea anemone to avoid being seen. Some sea anemones have round, sticky bumps called **verrucae** on their bodies. Bits of gravel, seashells, sand, and other materials stick to the verrucae and help a sea anemone to blend with its surroundings. This camouflage may actually have two purposes: It hides the anemone from predators, and it protects the anemone from the sun's rays.

Sometimes all defenses fail, and a sea anemone is attacked by a predator. When this happens, some anemones actually release their hold on the seafloor and try to escape from their attackers. Because sea anemones cannot move quickly, this defense only

Sea slugs like these, known as nudibranchs, prey on sea anemones.

An anemone feeds with its crimson tentacles extended (top) , while a closed anemone (bottom) hides its tentacles inside its upturned collar.

works against sea stars and other very slow-moving predators. However, fleeing can be a useful tactic when used as a last resort. Traveling just a tiny distance each minute, a sea anemone may stay ahead of its pursuer. By avoiding attack, the anemone will survive to hunt—and be hunted—another day.

chapter 21

Living Together

Most small ocean animals stay away from sea anemones because of their stinging tentacles. A few creatures, however, have found ways to take advantage of the sea anemone's venomous stingers. These creatures live with or even inside sea anemones. By doing so, they keep themselves safe from anemone-avoiding predators. At the same time, they give the anemone something it needs. These arrangements are examples of **mutualism**—a relationship between two creatures that helps both to survive.

Anemone Fish

The best-known sea anemone dwellers are undoubtedly the anemone fish, also called clown fish.

Anemone fish often have bright orange bodies with broad white and black stripes. Several of these colorful creatures may take up residence among the tentacles of a single sea anemone. This particular anemone will be the fishes' home for the rest of their lives. The anemone fish are very territorial and will dart out to attack any small animals that approach, thus protecting the sea anemone from creatures that might otherwise nibble on its column or tentacles. The anemone fish also help the sea anemone by creating waste products that can be eaten as food. In return, they are protected from larger predators by the sea anemone's venomous tentacles.

Creating Immunity

Anemone fish are not naturally immune to the sea anemone's sting. Before they set up housekeeping, they must create a relationship with an anemone by darting in and out of its tentacles for several hours. At first they let only tiny parts of the anemone's tentacles touch their bodies. This keeps the stings from overwhelming the fish. In time, the anemone fish gives off mucus that builds up in a thick coat all over its body. The mucus is a perfect chemical match to the host anemone, so it does not trigger the host's nematocysts. As long as the anemone fish lives within its host, it maintains its mucus coat and keeps its immunity. This protection does not, however, extend to other sea anemones. If an anemone

This anemone fish lives in safety among an anemone's venomous tentacles.

fish tries to enter another sea anemone—even one of the same species—without doing its immunity dance, it will be stung dead within minutes.

There are only ten types of sea anemones that host anemone fish. All are warm-water species. Many of these creatures are found in the waters of

Australia. They are also widespread throughout the South Pacific and Indian oceans, living anywhere from East Africa to Japan, Micronesia to Thailand. They are common in the Red Sea as well.

Crabs

Anemone fish are not the only creatures known for living with sea anemones. Hermit crabs are also well known for this behavior. These soft-bodied

A hermit crab with several anemones attached to its shell moves along the seafloor.

crabs protect themselves by living within the abandoned shells of other creatures. To add a little extra protection, they may encourage sea anemones to grow on the shells. They do this by massaging a living anemone until it releases its hold on rock or another hard base. The crabs then hold the anemones on top of their shells until the anemones attach themselves to their new home.

As a hermit crab gets bigger, from time to time it abandons its old shell and moves into a larger one. Some sea anemones leave the old shell on their own and follow the crab to its new home. Others need a little coaxing. The crab gently pulls an anemone loose from the abandoned shell, then holds it over the new shell until it reattaches itself.

A Good Partnership

Hermit crabs are not the only crabs that live with sea anemones. Boxer crabs, too, are often found together with these creatures. Boxer crabs hold small pom-pom–shaped sea anemones in their big front claws and carry them wherever they go. They wave the anemones to scare off large fish or any other predators that come too close. The boxer crab itself cannot be hurt because the sea anemone cannot sting the crab through its hard **exoskeleton**.

Sea anemones and crabs both benefit from their mutual living arrangements. A crab gets protection from a sea anemone, which scares off many animals that might like to eat the crab. In return, the sea anemone enjoys a continuous feast of floating food scraps dropped by the crab. The anemone is also able to move around and visit new areas—something that it would have great difficulty doing on its own. Traveling from place to place, the sea anemone gets all sorts of new foods and may have more opportunities to reproduce.

Algae

Some shallow-water sea anemones host teeming colonies of algae within their flesh. Called **zooxanthellae**, these algae live mostly within the sea anemone's oral disk and tentacles. Protected by their host's flesh, the algae bask safely in the rays of the sun. They take the sunlight into their bodies and use the energy to produce food for themselves. They also eat some of the sea anemone's waste products, such as nitrogen and phosphorus, and they breathe the carbon dioxide given off by the anemone. All of these things are important to the zooxanthellae's survival.

The host anemone gets a great deal from this living arrangement as well. The zooxanthellae dump edible waste products such as sugars into the sea anemone's body, thus keeping their host well fed. Also, by taking in their host's waste products, the zooxanthellae keep the anemone's environment clean and healthy. All in all, it is a good situation for the anemone, which has everything it needs to stay big and healthy even if food supplies drop.

Built to Survive

Zooxanthellae, crabs, and anemone fish are very important to their hosts. Many species of sea anemones that have adapted to live with these creatures have changed to the point that they could not survive on their own. However, these species are exceptions.

Some anemone species host vast colonies of algae hidden in their tentacles and oral disk.

Sea anemones like this one in the Philippines are hardy creatures that have existed for hundreds of millions of years.

Most sea anemones are not dependent on other animals. On the contrary, they are hardy creatures that can live in a wide variety of conditions and circumstances. Sea anemones and their ancestors have probably been on Earth for more than 500 million years, and there is no reason that they should not continue to thrive far into the future.

Glossary

Actiniaria: The scientific order to which all sea anemones belong.

Anthozoa: The scientific class to which all sea anemones belong.

basal disk: A pad at the bottom of the sea anemone's column.

camouflage: Coloration that helps a sea anemone to blend with its surroundings.

collar: A loose fold of flesh at the base of a sea anemone's tentacles.

column: A sea anemone's tubelike central body.

exoskeleton: A hard outer skeleton that surrounds and protects some creatures' bodies.

gastrovascular cavity: The hollow inside of a sea anemone's column.

larvae: The name given to sea anemones before they reach their adult form.

minyads: Sea anemones that float freely instead of holding on to a solid surface.

mutualism: A relationship in which two different species help each other.

nematocysts: Stinging structures that line a sea anemone's tentacles.

oral disk: A flat, fleshy area that tops a sea anemone's column. Contains the sea anemone's mouth.

planula: The name given to a sea anemone larva.

polyp: A general name for any creature with a hollow, tubelike body that is attached at one end and open at the other. The open end is usually surrounded by a ring of tentacles.

predators: Animals that hunt and eat other animals.

regeneration: The ability to grow an entire body from a small piece of flesh.

spawning: Releasing eggs and sperm into the water for the purpose of reproduction.

splitting: Reproducing by tearing the body in half. Each half develops into a whole animal.

tentacles: Flexible, fleshy structures that fringe the top of a sea anemone's column.

verrucae: Sticky bumps that line the columns of some sea anemones.

zooxanthellae: Algae that live within the flesh of some shallow-water sea anemones.

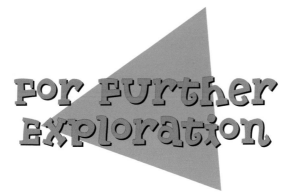

Books

Kris Hirschmann, *Coral.* San Diego, CA: KidHaven, 2005. Introduces one of the sea anemone's closest relatives.

Joyce Pope, *Deadly Venom: The World's Most Poisonous Animals.* Austin, TX: Steck-Vaughn Library, 1991. Discusses poisons in sea animals, insects, spiders, ambhibians, lizard, snakes, and mammals.

Alvin Silverstein, *Symbiosis.* Brookfield, CT: Twenty-First Century, 1998. Discusses the three kinds of symbiosis: mutualism, commensalism, and parasitism.

Philip Steele, *A Tidal Pool.* New York: Crabtree, 1999. Describes the different plants and animals that live in tidal pools at low, mid, and high tides.

John H. Tullock, *Clownfishes and Sea Anemones: Everything About Purchase, Care, Nutrition, Maintenance, and Setting Up an Aquarium.* Hauppage, NY: Barron's Educational Series, 1998. Provides all the information needed to keep clown fishes and sea anemones in a home aquarium.

Web Sites

Actiniaria (www.actiniaria.com). This site has a great collection of sea anemone images from all over the world.

Life in the Ocean (www.calstatela.edu/faculty/eviau/edit557/oceans/norma/oocean.htm). Learn about four ocean habitats—sandy beaches, tidal pools, kelp forests, and the open seas—and the animals that live in them.

Sea Anemone (www.enchantedlearning.com/subjects/invertebrates/seaanemone/Seaanemoneprintout.s html). This informational page includes a sea anemone diagram to print out and color.

index

picture credits

Cover photo: © Robert Yin/CORBIS
Gavin Anderson/Lonely Planet Images, 13
  (small)
Michael Aw/Lonely Planet Images, 35
© Jonathan Blair/CORBIS, 36
© Brandon D. Cole/CORBIS, 32 (top)
Jenny and Tony Enderby/Lonely Planet Images,
  7, 11 (large)
Jamie Hall/NOAA, 31 (top)
© W. Wayne Lockwood, M.D./CORBIS, 13
  (large)
Casey and Astrid Witte Mahaney, 9
PhotoDisc, 11 (small)
© Jeffrey L. Rotman/CORBIS, 16, 26, 28, 39
Mark Webster/Lonely Planet Images, 31
  (bottom)
© Stuart Westmorland/CORBIS, 19, 32
  (bottom)
© Douglas P. Wilson; Frank Lane Picture
  Agency/CORBIS, 20, 24
© Lawson Wood/CORBIS, 23
© Robert Yin/CORBIS, 14, 40

about the author

Kris Hirschmann has written more than one hundred books for children. She is the president of The Wordshop, a business that provides a variety of writing and editorial services. She holds a bachelor's degree in psychology from Dartmouth College in Hanover, New Hampshire.

Hirschmann lives just outside Orlando, Florida, with her husband, Michael, and her daughters, Nikki and Erika.